20 DECREES & DECLARATIONS FOR WOMEN

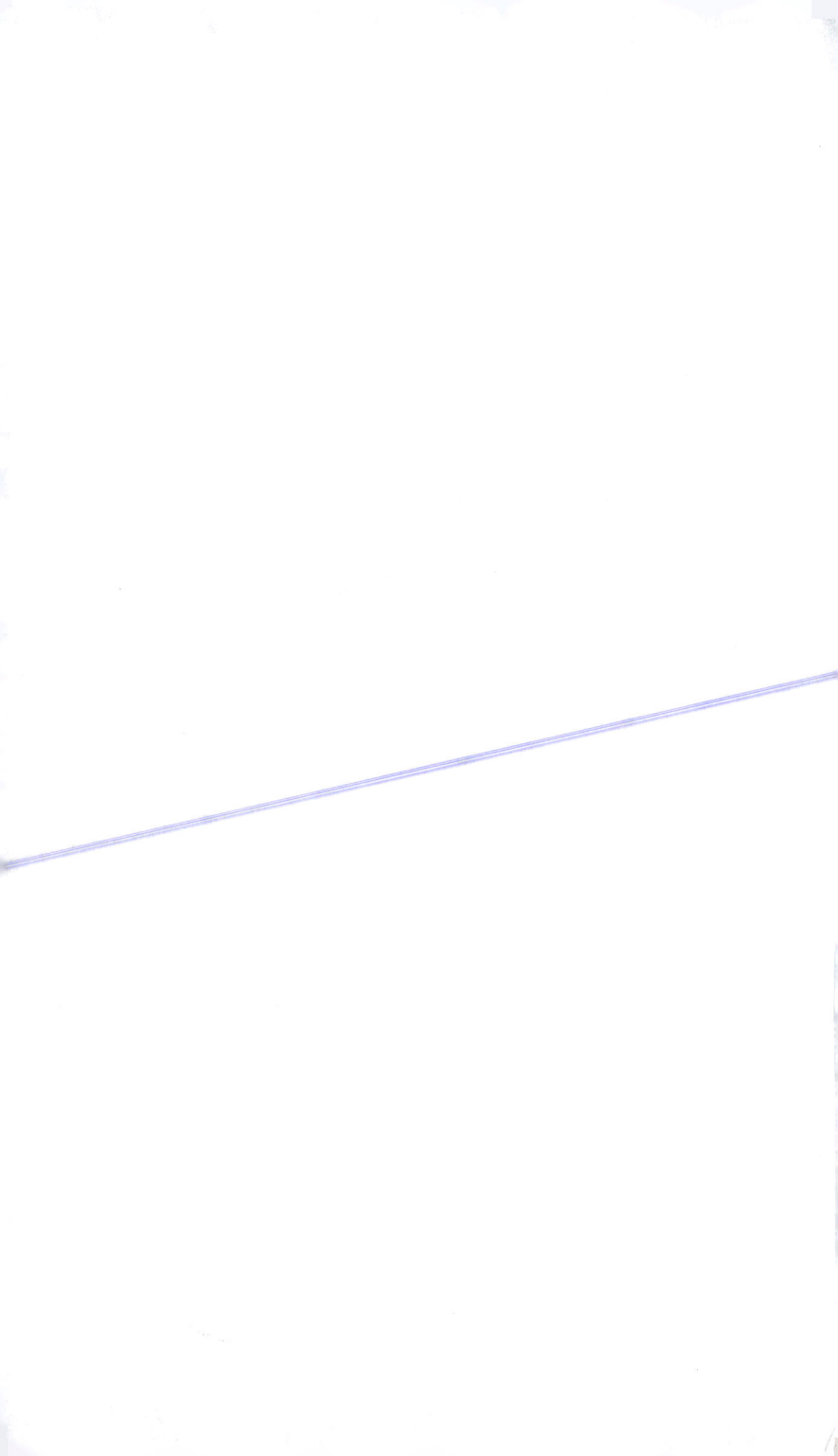

TWENTY
decrees & declarations
FOR WOMEN

THE POWER OF GOD'S
WORD AND THE POWER OF
YOUR VOICE

DIANE E. SANDERS

Palmetto Publishing Group
Charleston, SC

20 Decrees & Declarations for Women
Copyright © 2020 by Diane E. Sanders
All rights reserved

No portion of this book may be reproduced, stored in a retrieval system, or transmitted in any form by any means–electronic, mechanical, photocopy, recording, or other except for brief quotations in printed reviews, without prior permission of the author.

First Edition

Printed in the United States

ISBN-13: 978-1-64990-070-8
ISBN-10: 1-64990-070-8

This book is dedicated to my daughter, Courtney, for her love and support and her faithfulness through this journey and throughout our life's journey together; to my brother, David, for his steadfast love and support and his constant reminder that no matter where I am in my life's journey, I am not alone, but rather we are in it together; and to my friends and sisterhood who encouraged me to publish this book.

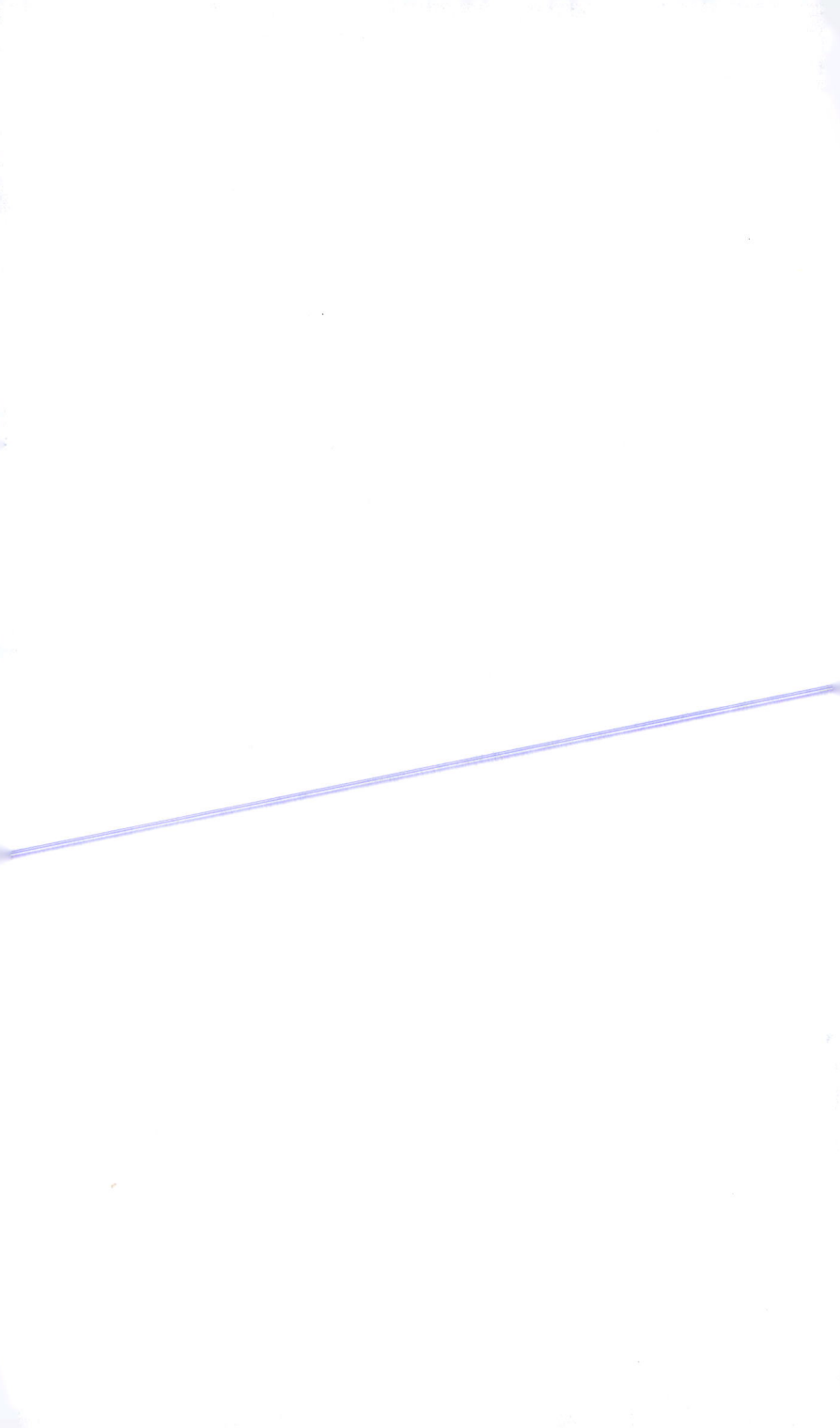

CONTENTS

Contents	vii
Introduction	1
Definitions	3
Who Am I?	4
Health and Healing	8
Favor	12
Wisdom	16
Provision	20
Family and Friends	24
Protection	28
Peace	32
Fear	36
Love	40
Forgiveness	44
Holy Spirit	48
Courage	52
Rest	56
Confidence	60
Hope	64
Worry and Anxiety	68
Faith	72
Joy	76
Praise	80
Scriptural References	85
About the Author	89

INTRODUCTION

I was inspired to write this book of decrees and declarations from my personal experience of years reading, meditating, and speaking aloud many of these scriptures and quotes. As I continued to do this, I began to see God's Word being activated and transforming my life.

I have taken twenty topics I believe many women have questions about and challenges with throughout the different seasons in life. I begin these decrees and declarations with what I think are the predominate areas with which women struggle—knowing and recognizing their identity in Christ, and having confidence as they navigate through life.

God has created each of us with a purpose and destiny to fulfill while we are on the earth regardless of our season in life. Whatever God has entrusted you to do regardless of your season in life, you can do it through Christ. When you know your identity, it is then you gain and own your confidence. For your true identity comes from Christ!

decrees & declarations

These decrees and declarations are scriptures from the Bible and written in the first person so you can personalize them. I believe as you speak aloud and meditate on these faith-filled, life-giving decrees and declarations, they will become personal and transform you as well.

- Job 22:28 says, "You shall decree a thing, and it shall be established unto you."
- Proverbs 18:21 says, "Life and death is in the power of your tongue and those who love it will eat its fruit."
- 2 Corinthians 4:13 says, "We believe therefore we spoke, and I believe therefore I speak."

What better way to start your day by speaking aloud and meditating on these decrees and declarations to renew and transform your mind, your health, your relationships, your spiritual well-being and your life?

DEFINITIONS

decree.
an authoritative order or decision;
to command

declaration.
a formal statement; an announcement;
a proclamation

WHO AM I?

I am fearfully and wonderfully made;
Marvelous are your works
—Psalms 139:143

I DECREE AND DECLARE TODAY

I am a daughter of the Most High God, created in my father's imagine.

I am chosen, I am accepted, I am deeply loved, I am highly favored, and I am greatly blessed in Christ.

I am the righteous of God in Christ.

I am filled with the Holy Spirit, who leads me, guides me, and empowers me into all truths.

I am wise because Jesus has made unto me wisdom.

I am healed and whole—spirit, soul, and body through Christ.

I am creative, successful, and prosperous through Christ.

JOURNAL YOUR THOUGHTS

decrees & declarations

I am a gracious woman and a woman of honor, virtue, strength, and integrity through Christ.

I am free to be all that God has called me to be through Christ.

I am an over comer and more than a conqueror through Christ. I will run my race, finish my course, keep the faith, and attain my God-given purpose and destiny through Christ.

I am a woman of great influence in the kingdom of God.

I am who my Father God says I am!

JOURNAL YOUR THOUGHTS

HEALTH AND HEALING

Beloved, I pray that you may prosper in all things and be in health, just as your soul prospers.
—3 John 1:2

I DECREE AND DECLARE TODAY

As my days are, so shall my strength be.

My spirit is strong, my mind is sharp, my emotions are calm, and my body is healed.

God, You, have sent Your word and healed me and redeemed my life from destruction.

Jesus has come with healing in his wings, and by his stripes I am healed!

God, Your word is life and health for my whole body.

I have a happy and grateful heart and a cheerful mind that brings forth healing to me.

JOURNAL YOUR THOUGHTS

decrees & declarations

The joy of the Lord is my strength, and it brings me physical, emotional, and mental healing.

Jesus heals the brokenhearted and binds up all my emotional and mental wounds.

My youth is renewed like an eagle, and with long life the Lord satisfies me and shows me his salvation.

I am like a tree that stays healthy and fruitful even in old age.

JOURNAL YOUR THOUGHTS

FAVOR

For he who finds me finds life; and obtains favor from the Lord.
—Proverbs 8:35

I DECREE AND DECLARE TODAY

Favor surrounds me like a shield.

God's favor on my life is more valuable than silver and gold.

I am growing daily in wisdom, stature, and favor with God and with others.

The favor of God on my life causes me to be steady as a mountain.

God's favor on my life endures for a lifetime and causes even my enemies to favor me.

I have favor in all that I do. Doors of opportunities are opening unto me; and resources come into my hands from the north, south, east, and west in the most supernatural ways.

JOURNAL YOUR THOUGHTS

decrees & declarations

The Lord favors me and establishes all the works of my hands.

God favors and honors me, and no good thing will He withhold from me as I walk uprightly.

God, You guide my footsteps along the right path and grant me favor.

I have favor everywhere I go!

JOURNAL YOUR THOUGHTS

WISDOM

*Through wisdom a house is built, and
by understanding it is established;*
—Proverbs 24:3

I DECREE AND DECLARE TODAY

Wisdom is the principle thing for my life, and I have access to wisdom when I ask You, Father God, and You give it to me generously..

I receive wisdom that comes from above, which is first pure, peaceable, gentle, open to reason, full of mercy, good fruit, and impartial.

I am the righteous of God in Christ, and the mouth of the righteous flows with wisdom.

Because the mind of Christ lives in me, I have the wisdom, knowledge, understanding, insights, and solutions that I need in any situation and circumstance.

JOURNAL YOUR THOUGHTS

decrees & declarations

I look carefully at how I walk, living purposefully and honorably, not as the unwise but as a wise, sensible, and intelligent woman.

As I walk with wise women, I become wise, and the Lord teaches me to use my time wisely.

Skillful and godly wisdom is from the Lord, and from You, Lord, I receive knowledge and understanding.

Wisdom is better than gold and understanding better than silver. And both riches and honor are in my hands.

I will listen to good counsel, receive instructions, and accept correction that I may be wise.

O Lord, teach me to consider my days that I may gain a heart of wisdom.

JOURNAL YOUR THOUGHTS

PROVISION

The Lord is my shepherd I shall not want.
—Psalms 23:1

I DECREE AND DECLARE TODAY

God supplies all my needs according to his riches in glory by Christ Jesus.

God, You provide for me in ways that are exceedingly, abundantly above all that I can ask, think, or imagine.

I will not fail, I will not come up short, I will not lack, I will not want, I will not be diminished, and I will not fear!

God, You are my source for everything that I need, and it is You who gives me the ability to produce wealth.

God takes pleasure in prospering me in my spirit, soul, mind, and body and every area of my life.

God is blessing me abundantly in all things and at all times that I will have all that I need to do every good work that he has planned for me.

JOURNAL YOUR THOUGHTS

decrees & declarations

I will remember that it is You, God, who gives me creative, innovative, and resourceful ideals that I may prosper and succeed.

As I give, it will be given unto me; good measure, pressed down, shaken together, and running over will others give unto me.

I seek first the kingdom of God and his righteousness, and all these things will be added to me.

I am blessed to be a blessing in Jesus' name!

JOURNAL YOUR THOUGHTS

FAMILY AND FRIENDS

Behold, how good and how pleasant it is for brethren to dwell together in unity.
—Psalms 133:1

I DECREE AND DECLARE TODAY

My family dwells together in unity and love. Our relationship with one another is good and pleasant, and we are blessed.

All my children and grandchildren shall be taught of the Lord, and great shall be their peace.

My family is walking in the light of God's love, and we are made strong through His love.

All of my family will walk in all the works God has prepared for us from before the foundation of the world.

Clear and good communication and reasoning flow in my family, and the Holy Spirit imparts God-given understanding toward one another.

FAMILY AND FRIENDS

JOURNAL YOUR THOUGHTS

decrees & declarations

I am blessed beyond measure with wonderful life-giving family, friends, and relationships.

No greater love has anyone than to willingly lay down their life for a friend. And Jesus is that friend who sticks closer to me than a brother.

I have been graced to be a good friend who loves at all times.

My friends and I are not quarrelsome toward one another, but we are kind, patient, and respectful to one another.

I love my friends for they are gifts from God.

Family and Friends

JOURNAL YOUR THOUGHTS

PROTECTION

*For he shall give his angels charge over
thee to keep thee in all thy ways.
—Psalms 91:11*

I DECREE AND DECLARE TODAY

No weapon formed against me will prosper, and every tongue that rises up against me in judgment I will condemn. And God will vindicate me!

No evil will overtake me, and no plague or calamity will come near my dwelling. (Psalm 91:6-7)

The Lord will keep me safe from deadly pestilence. You will cover me with Your feathers, and under Your wings, I will find refuge. (Psalm 91:3-4)

God has commanded His angels to protect me and keep me wherever I go. (Psalm 91:11)

At times I may have troubles, but I will call out to You, Lord, and You deliver me. (Psalm 91:15)

JOURNAL YOUR THOUGHTS

decrees & declarations

The angel of the Lord encamps around about me and protects me.

The name of the Lord is a strong tower where the righteous run into, and I am safe.

When I call on the Lord, He answers me; and He rescues me and shows me His salvation.

Lord, You are my shield and fortress, and my place of safety. You will never leave me nor forsake me.

I am not afraid, for I put my trust in You, God. And I will trust You to deliver me from every hidden trap.

PROTECTION

JOURNAL YOUR THOUGHTS

PEACE

Peace I leave with you, my peace I give unto you: not as the world gives, give I unto you.
—John 14:27

I DECREE AND DECLARE TODAY

I am not anxious about anything, but with thanksgiving, I make my request known to You, God, and Your peace that passes all my understanding and reasoning will guard my heart and mind.

God guides my feet into the way of peace, and I will live peaceably with everyone as much as it depends on me.

I am a peacemaker who sows in peace, and I will reap a harvest of righteousness.

I pursue the things that make for peace and building up of others.

The Lord lifts up his countenance upon me and give me peace.

JOURNAL YOUR THOUGHTS

decrees & declarations

Because I love God's instructions, I have great peace, and I will not be offended.

Grace and peace have been multiplied to me in the knowledge of God and of Jesus Christ, my Lord.

I will listen carefully to all that the Lord is saying to me, for He speaks peace.

The work of righteousness is peace, and the results of righteousness are quietness and confidence.

Christ is my peace and my well-being.

JOURNAL YOUR THOUGHTS

FEAR

Fear not, little flock, for it is your Father's good pleasure to give you the Kingdom.
—*Luke 12:32*

I DECREE AND DECLARE TODAY

God has not given me a spirit of fear but of power, love, and sound mind.

I will not be frightened; nor will I be dismayed for the Lord has gone before me.

I will not let my heart be troubled or stressed; neither will I be afraid.

I will not fear for the Lord God is upholding me with His victorious right hand.

I will not be afraid or terrified of them for the Lord is with me.

JOURNAL YOUR THOUGHTS

decrees & declarations

I do not fear for the steps of a righteous woman are directed of the Lord, and You, Lord, delight in every step I take, and I am strengthened.

When I am afraid, I will trust in You, God, in Whom I am made strong by the power of the Holy Spirit.

Lord, You are my light and my salvation, so why should I fear?

I trust in You, Lord, with all my heart and I lean not on my own understanding or reasoning. In all my ways, I will submit to You, and You will make my paths straight.

I will not fear for You, Lord, are strengthening.

JOURNAL YOUR THOUGHTS

LOVE

For God is Love.
—1 John 4:8

I DECREE AND DECLARE TODAY

I love God because He first loved me.

I am loved with God's everlasting love, and nothing can separate me from Your love.

I will love You, God, with all my heart, my soul, and all that is within me, and I will love my neighbor as I love myself.

God, Your love and kindness are better to me than life itself. Oh, how I praise You!

God, Your love has been shed abroad in my heart by the Holy Spirit.

I will put on love that binds everything together in perfect harmony.

JOURNAL YOUR THOUGHTS

decrees & declarations

I will walk in love toward others this day, for love is patient, kind, not envious, arrogant, rude or resentful, and it does not insist on its own way. And love will never fail.

If I speak with the eloquence of many languages and in heavenly tongues of angels and yet I do not express myself with love, my words are as an empty hollow clanging cymbal.

My love will be sincere and real. I will hate evil and all wrongdoing, but I will hold fast to that which is good and right.

Faith, hope, and love dwell in me, but the greatest of these is love. And my faith works by my love in Jesus' name!

JOURNAL YOUR THOUGHTS

FORGIVENESS

And when you stand praying, forgive, if you have an ought against anyone, that your Father in heaven may also forgive you your trespasses.
—Mark 11:25

I DECREE AND DECLARE TODAY

God, I will forgive those who have wronged me, as You have forgiven me for those whom I have wronged.

I confess my faults, slips, offenses, and mistakes to another, and pray for one another that we may be healed emotionally and mentally and restored.

O Lord, search my heart and test my motives to see if there are any wicked ways in me. Create in me a clean heart and renew a right spirit within me.

I will not hold a grudge or try to get even with anyone, but I will purposely live my life in a way that is honorable and benefit others.

JOURNAL YOUR THOUGHTS

decrees & declarations

I am kind, compassionate, and forgiving of others, as God through Christ have forgiven me.

If I have a grievance or conflict against another, I will leave my gift of offerings at the altar and go and be reconciled that my gift of offerings will be accepted and my prayers answered.

I will not be judgmental, critical, or condemning of others, but rather I will extend grace and love as God has extended his grace and love toward me.

I choose to forgive and release anyone that I have an offense or un-forgiveness toward as You, Holy Spirit, reveal them to me.

I will love my enemies, do good to them, pray for them, and forgive them as God, You, has forgiven me.

Because I have been blessed and given grace and mercy, I will give grace and mercy toward others. For to whom much is given, much is required.

JOURNAL YOUR THOUGHTS

HOLY SPIRIT

And I will pray the Father, and he shall give you another Comforter, that he may abide with you forever.
—John 14:16

I DECREE AND DECLARE TODAY

When He, the Spirit of truth, comes, He will guide me into all truth, for He will not speak on His own authority but what He hears from the Father, and He will tell me of things to come.

The same Spirit that raised Christ from the dead lives in me and brings life, health, and wholeness to my body.

I have anointing from the Holy One that I have been set apart, specially gifted, and prepared by the Holy Spirit Who teaches me.

The works that I do is not in my own strength or power but in the authority and power of the Holy Spirit.

JOURNAL YOUR THOUGHTS

decrees & declarations

I will build myself up on my most holy faith, praying in the Holy Spirit.

I will speak with other tongues as the Spirit gives me utterance.

I will receive power when the Holy Spirit comes upon me to be a witness.

I have the fruit of the Spirit living within me, which is love, joy, peace, patience, kindness, goodness, faithfulness, gentleness, and self-control.

The Holy Spirit is resting on me today, and he provides his wisdom, his help, and his comfort.

The Lord is the Spirit, and where the Spirit of the Lord is there is freedom.

JOURNAL YOUR THOUGHTS

COURAGE

Be on your guard; stand firm in the faith; be courageous; be strong.
—1 Corinthians 16:13

I DECREE AND DECLARE TODAY

My heart is strong and courageous.

I will not lose my courage because it has a great reward for me.

I am bold and courageous because the Lord God is with me. He will never leave me or forsake me.

I encourage myself daily in God's Word, and with songs of hymns I will praise him!

I draw near to the throne of grace with boldness, and I receive mercy and find grace for help in my time of need.

The joy of the Lord is my strength, and the glory and lifter of my head.

JOURNAL YOUR THOUGHTS

decrees & declarations

I am strong and courageous because I am the righteous in Christ, and the righteous are bold as a lion.

I will stand firm and let nothing move me. I will give myself fully to the work of the Lord, knowing that my labor will not be in vain.

I am strong in the Lord and in the power of His might. I put on the whole armor of God that I may be able to stand against the schemes of the devil.

I will take courage for the Lord God is with me!

JOURNAL YOUR THOUGHTS

REST

He leads me besides still waters
and He restores my soul.
—Psalms 23:2

I DECREE AND DECLARE TODAY

When I am weary and overwhelmed, I go to You, Lord, and You give me rest for my body, mind, and emotions.

I will be still and rest in God and see His goodness and faithfulness in the land of the living.

God, You, let me rest in green meadows. You lead me beside peaceful streams, and You renew my strength.

Because I dwell in the shelter of the Most High, I will rest in the shadow of the Almighty.

I will walk in the ways of the Lord and find rest for my mind and soul.

JOURNAL YOUR THOUGHTS

decrees & declarations

I will cease from striving and pause and know that you are God!

I will rest in the Lord and wait patiently for him.

Lord. You, lead by Your presence, and give me rest.

Lord, You give me Your beloved sweet sleep and rest.

I will remember the sabbath day and rest.

JOURNAL YOUR THOUGHTS

CONFIDENCE

The Lord shall be my confidence.
—Proverbs 3:26

I DECREE AND DECLARE TODAY

I know with great confidence that, God, You are concerned about me. And You cause all things to work together for good, because I love You, and I am called according to Your plan and purpose.

I am confident of this very thing, that You, God, who has begun a good work in me, will perform it until the day of Jesus Christ.

I am God's handiwork, created in Christ Jesus to do good works, which God has prepared in advance for me to do. And I can do it!

This is the confidence that I have in You, God, that if I ask anything according to Your will, You hear and answer me.

JOURNAL YOUR THOUGHTS

decrees & declarations

I have confidence in You, God, Who is my strength.

In reverence and worshipful honor of You, Lord, I find my confidence and my security.

I will examine myself and the work that I do, and I will not compare myself with someone else.

Strength and dignity are my clothing, and my position is strong and secure; therefore, I will smile at my future.

O Lord, You have been my confidence and my hope since I was young; and my songs of praise constantly speak about You.

I am a blessed woman because my trust and confidence is in You, Lord.

JOURNAL YOUR THOUGHTS

HOPE

Hope deferred makes the heart sick, but when the desire comes it is a tree of life.
—Proverbs 13:12

I DECREE AND DECLARE TODAY

Lord, You know the plans that You have for me; they are plans for good and not for harm, to give me a future and a hope.

I will hold fast to my confession of my hope without wavering, knowing that, God, You cannot lie because You, Who has promised are faithful.

When I run into problems and trials, I can rejoice for I know that they help me develop endurance, and endurance develops strength of character. Character strengthens confidence, and confidence strengthens my hope. And this hope does not disappoint me.

Lord, I put my hope in You and you alone; therefore my hope will not be cut off.

JOURNAL YOUR THOUGHTS

decrees & declarations

My soul says, "Lord, You are my portion and my inheritance; therefore, I have hope in You and wait expectantly for You".

May the God of *hope* fill me with all joy and peace in believing that by the power of the Holy Spirit I will abound in *hope.*

Lord, my soul longs for Your salvation, and I have put my hope in Your word.

I will not put my hope in money or the uncertainty of riches but in God, who gives richly all things for me to enjoy.

I have a hope that anchors my soul, and that hope is in the Lord Jesus Christ!

I will rejoice in hope, be patient in tribulation, and be constant in prayer.

JOURNAL YOUR THOUGHTS

WORRY AND ANXIETY

"I tell you not to worry about everyday life—whether you have enough food and drink, or enough clothes to wear. Isn't life more than food and your body more than clothing? Look at the birds. They don't plant or harvest or store food in barns, for your heavenly Father feeds them. And aren't you far more valuable to him than they are? Can all your worries add a single moment to your life"?
—Matthew 6:25-27

I DECREE AND DECLARE TODAY

I will not be anxious for anything, but in everything by prayer and supplication, with thanksgiving, I will make my requests known to You, God.

I will cast all my anxiety on You, Lord, because You care for me.

I will say, if God be for me, who can be against me?

I will not let my heart be trouble. In Jesus name!

JOURNAL YOUR THOUGHTS

decrees & declarations

I will not worry beforehand how I will answer or defend myself. For You, Lord, will give me the right words and wisdom that none of my adversaries will oppose me or say that I am wrong.

I choose to fix my thoughts on whatever is true and good and right; and on things that are pure and lovely, and of a good report. I will think about all that I can praise You, God, for and rejoice.

I will stop worrying about tomorrow, for tomorrow will bring its own worries.

The temptations in my life are no different from what others experience, and God is faithful. He will not allow the temptation to be more than I can stand; and He will show me a way out that I can endure.

I will not hold anxiety in my heart, because it weighs my heart down.

I will trust in the Lord with all my heart and lean not on my own understanding. In all my ways I will acknowledge You, and You will direct my paths.

JOURNAL YOUR THOUGHTS

FAITH

"For by grace you have been saved through faith. And this is not your own doing; it is the gift of God, not a result of works, so that no one may boast.
—Ephesians 2: 8-9

I DECREE AND DECLARE TODAY

My faith is the assurance of things I hope for, the evidence of things I cannot see.

Jesus, You said if I have faith as small as a mustard seed, I can say to my mountain to move and do not doubt in my heart it will go; and nothing will be impossible for me.

My faith comes by hearing and hearing through the word of God. For nothing is impossible with God.

My faith does not rest in my wisdom but in the power of God.

JOURNAL YOUR THOUGHTS

decrees & declarations

Lord, because I believe in You as the scriptures have said" Rivers of living water will flow from my inner most being".

Lord, You have said that whatever I ask in prayer according to Your word I will receive if I have faith.

I am the righteousness of God in Christ, and the righteous live by faith.

I will walk by faith, not by sight today!

I choose the way of faithfulness and I have set my heart on Your word.

I will fight the good fight, I will finish my race, and I will keep the Faith!

JOURNAL YOUR THOUGHTS

JOY

*"The Joy of the Lord is my strength.
—Nehemiah 8:10*

I DECREE AND DECLARE TODAY

Lord, You have made known to me the path of life, and in Your presence is fullness of joy.

Weeping may last through the night, but joy will come to me with the morning.

Lord, Your precepts are right and bring joy to my heart.

As I look to You, Lord, for help I will radiate with joy; and my face will not be shamed.

Oh, the joys I have because I do not follow the advice of the wicked, but I delight in the word of the Lord. I meditate on it day and night. I will be like a tree planted by streams of water and bearing fruit in each season. I will prosper in all that I do.

JOURNAL YOUR THOUGHTS

decrees & declarations

Because I please You, God, You give me wisdom, knowledge, and joy.

I will come into Your presence, Lord, with thanksgiving. I will make a joyful noise to You, with songs of praise!

As I keep Your commandments, Lord, I will abide in Your love; and Your joy shall be in me and my joy will be made full.

I will delight myself in You, Lord; and You will give me the desires of my heart.

JOURNAL YOUR THOUGHTS

PRAISE

Let everything that has breath praise the L‍ORD! Praise the L‍ORD.
—*Psalms 150:6*

I DECREE AND DECLARE TODAY

I will bless the Lord at all times. His praise will continually be in my mouth.

It is good for me to give thanks to You, Lord, to sing praises to Your name, O Most High. I declare Your steadfast love in the morning and Your faithfulness at night.

All day long I'll praise and honor You, God; for all that You have done for me.

I will praise You, God, for Your mighty acts and praise You according to Your excellent greatness.

I will praise the Lord, O my soul, and all that is within me. I will praise Your holy name!

JOURNAL YOUR THOUGHTS

decrees & declarations

I will praise You, Lord, for You are good, and Your loving-kindness and mercy endure forever.

For great is the Lord and greatly to be praised. And every day I will praise You.

I will thank You, God, forever and ever, praising Your greatness from generation to generation.

I will rejoice in the Lord, and I will be happy in the God of my salvation.

I will rejoice in You, Lord, always, and again I say Rejoice!

JOURNAL YOUR THOUGHTS

SCRIPTURAL REFERENCES

"Who Am I?": Gen. 1:27; Eph. 1:11, 6; Eph. 2:4; Luke 1:28; 2 Cor. 5:21; John. 16:13; 1Cor. 1:30; Isa. 53:3; Prov. 11:16; Prov. 31:10; Prov. 31:17, 31:29 -30; 2 Peter 1:10, 12:11; Heb. 12:1; Esther 4:14

"Health and Healing": Deut. 33:25; Ps. 107:20; Mal. 4:2, Isa. 53:5; Prov. 4:22, 17:22; Neh. 8:10; Ps. 147:3, 103:5, 91:16, 92:14.

"Favor": Ps. 5:12; Prov. 22:1; Luke 2:52: Ps. 30:7, 30:5; Rom. 16:7; Ps. 90:17; Ps. 84:11; Prov. 5:10; Ps. 5:12

"Provision": Phil. 4:1; Eph. 3:20; Ps. 23:1; Matt. 10:28; Deut. 8:18; Ps.35:27; 2 Cor. 9:8; Prov. 8: 11-12; Josh. 1:8; Luke 6:38; Matt. 6:33; Zep.8:13

"Wisdom": Prov.4:7; James1:5, 3:17; Prov. 10:3; 2 Cor.5:21; Phil. 2:5; Col. 1:9; Eph. 5:15; Prov. 13:20; Prov. 6:16; Prov. 19:20; Ps. 90:12

"Family and Friends": Ps. 133:1; Isa. 54:13; Eph. 2:10; John 15:13; Prov. 17:17; 2 Tim. 2:24

decrees & declarations

"Protection": Isa. 54:17; Ps. 91:10; Ps.91:3-4; Ps. 91:11; Ps. 34:19; Ps. 34:7; Prov.18:10; Ps. 91:15-16; Ps. 91:2; Ps. 91:3

"Peace": Phil. 4:6, 7; Luke 1:79; Rom. 12:18; James 3:18; Rom. 14:19; Num. 6:26; Ps. 119:165; 2 Pet. 1:2; Ps. 85:8; Isa. 32:17; Eph. 2:14.

"Forgiveness": Matt. 6:14; James 5:16; Ps. 139:24; Ps.51:10; Lev.19:18; Eph. 4:32; Matt. 5:24; Luke 6:37; Luke 6:27; Heb.4:16; Luke 12:48

"Love": John 4:19; Jer. 31:3; Matt. 22: 37-38; Ps. 63:3; Rom. 6:6; Col. 3:14; 1 Cor. 13:4; 1 Cor. 13:4; 1 Cor. 13:1; Rom. 12:9; 1 Cor. 13:13

"Fear": 2 Tim. 1:7; Josh. 1:9; John 14:27; Isa. 41:10; Deut.31:16; Ps. 37:23; Ps. 56:3; Ps. 27:1; Prov. 3:5-6; Isa. 41:10

"Holy Spirit": John 16:13; Rom. 8:11; 1 John 2:20; John 14:10; Jude: 20; Act. 2:4; Act. 1:8; Gal. 5:22-23; Isa. 11:2; 2 Cor. 3:17

"Courage": Ps. 31:24; Heb.10:35; Deut. 31:6; Col. 3:16; Heb. 4:16; Neh. 8:10; Ps. 3:3; Prov. 28:1;

Scriptural References

1 Cor. 15:58; Eph. 6:16; Matt. 14:27

"Rest": Matt. 11:28; Ps. 46:10; Ps. 23:2–3; Ps. 91:1; Jer. 6:16; Ps. 37:7; Exod. 33:14; Ps. 127:2; Gen. 2:3.

"Confidence": Rom. 8:28; Phil.1: 6; Eph. 2:10; 1 John 5:14; Ps.139:24; Ps. 71:5; Ps. 105:2; Jer. 17:7

"Hope": Jer. 29:11; Heb. 10:23; Rom. 5:3–5; Ps. 62:5; Prov. 23:18; Lam. 3:24; Rom. 15:13; Ps. 119:81; 1 Tim. 6:17; Heb. 6:19; Rom. 12:12.

"Worry and Anxiety": Phil. 4:6; 1 Peter 5:7; Rom. 8:31; Luke 21:14-15; John 14:1; Phil. 4:8; Matt. 6:34; Prov. 12:25; 1 Cor.10:13; Prov. 3:5-6

"Faith": Heb. 11:1; Mark 11:23; Rom.10:7; Luke 1:37; 1 Cor. 2:5; John 7:38; Matt. 17:20; Rom. 1:7; 2 Cor. 5:7; Ps. 119:30; 2 Tim. 4:7

"Joy": Ps.16:11; Ps. 30:5; Ps. 19:8; Ps. 34:5; Ps. 1:1-3; Ecce. 2:26; Ps. 95:2; John 15:11; Ps. 37:4; Ps. 4:4

"Praise": Ps. 34:1. 92:1–2, 71:8, 150:2, 103:1, 106:1, 45:1, 79:13; Hab. 3:18; Phil. 4:4.

ABOUT THE AUTHOR

Diane E. Sanders is a health and wholeness consultant and coach, nutritionist, author, speaker and founder of Living Strong After 50 LLC. She holds a B.A. in psychology specializing in health and advance training certification in nutrition. Diane's passion is to educate, equip and support women and men who have entered the second half of life to live a healthy, healed, purposeful and whole life–mind, body and spirit. To find out more, go to www.livingstrongafter50.com.